First published by TC Publishing 2021

Portia Ruzario asserts the moral right to be identified as the author of this work.

ISBN 978-1-9163764-5-8

PUBLISHING

Contents Page

Intro   10-11

My story   12-17

More than a chicken dream   18-20

Chicken a healthy choice   21

Equipment for preparing, storing, and cooking chicken 22-26

Essential dry store ingredients 27-28

Preparation is key to success in life 28-34

More than one way to cook a chicken   35-38

Kitchen tips   39

My favourite inspirational quotes   40

Recipes   41

Examples of chicken menus   42

Base recipes   43-46

Ginger, honey & soy chicken   47-48

Pesto chicken   49-50

Parmesan chicken   51-52

Thai flavoured grilled spatchcock chicken   53-54

Fried chicken   55-56

Roast chicken 1.6 – 1.8 kg   57-58

Sunshine chicken   59-60

Salt and pepper chicken   61-63

Jerk style chicken   64-65

Chicken curry – flavours of Bahia   66-67

Braised red pepper & tomato chicken   68-69

Lemon & herb chicken   70-71

BBQ chicken   72-73

Malay chicken curry   74-75

Peri Peri chicken   76-77

Cajun chicken   78-79

Harissa chicken   80-81

Butter chicken curry (makhani)   82-84

Warm chicken & orzo salad   85-86

Chicken tikka   87-88

Chicken Yassa   89-91

Chipotle chicken   92-93

Chicken fajitas   94-95

Pot roast chicken   96-98

White chicken casserole   99-100

Conclusion   101-102

Notes   103-104

Index   105-108

Foreword by Chikumo Fiseko

As I write this, I have been working with Portia for a few months to put this book together amongst other mini projects.

As a general foodie and a food stylist, my life revolves around food. It's also how my family and I bond.

From this book I have already recreated a few recipes which have been extremely popular with my family! I love how simple they are to make, but I also love how they leave room for creativeness. For example, we had roasted chicken with mac 'n' cheese and homemade coleslaw. I would have normally just bought the coleslaw, but I wanted to make it all from scratch and that's what I love about the book. It just adds to my love of fresh food.

This book has also opened doors I felt were shut because of COVID 19 restrictions, and it has allowed me to awaken the creativity inside me. Not just by putting this book together, but by allowing me to play with the recipes and style them as practice for myself. Getting to eat the amazing chicken dishes has been an added bonus.

I'm slowly making my way through the recipes and so far, I haven't had one complaint. I cannot wait to try the rest. I implore you to join me on the Chicken Inn journey and share your creations with us!

Chikumo Fiseko
Food & Marketing Consultant
www.chikumofiseko.com

About the book

This book is more than just a cookery book with enticing chicken recipes. It's a book that seeks to inspire the reader to leave the hen house and fly like an eagle. It has captivating stories, quotes and practical lessons on how to improve life by association, creativity, resilience, preparation and investing in simple tools and ingredients to create a better future.

It will challenge the reader to *marinate* and *season* an idea till the flavours intensify. After the process of marination and cooking, the celebration begins for the worthy wait. It will also motivate the reader to shift their mindset, pursue their dream and develop and encourage themselves in the journey of life. You will never look at a chicken in the same way again when you make the *decision* to build your 'Chicken Inn' and not Chicken Out!

Acknowledgements

I would like to thank Chikumo, for her hard work, attention to detail and for inspiring me. Writing this book wouldn't have been possible had I not flown in her zone.

I thank my husband, Terence, for supporting me on the writing journey and believing in me.

I thank my children, Terry, Hannah and Naomi for cheering me on.

I thank my friends, family, and customers for the opportunity to keep cooking and perfecting the chicken dishes.

Last, but not least, I thank Tarnya and her publishing company for assisting me in the completion of my book. A great learning point in the writing journey is to always reach out to those already flying.

Preface

To fast track your dream, you must imagine it is real before you can touch it. You must season and marinate it in your mind with quality spices and herbs, and then you will reap flavourful results after some time. Believe you can! Speak to your senses and whet your appetite to taste your dream. Soon, the aroma of what's cooking will saturate your atmosphere and the feast will begin.

When my mind and surroundings scream, I can't have my dream, I say, "YES, CHIC-KEN!" (yes, she can

Introduction

We are living in unprecedented times. Our country and nations worldwide have been impacted by the deadly Corona Virus. Countries have been on 'lockdown' since March 2020 to slow down and eliminate this COVID-19 virus which has claimed many lives. Most places of work have since shut down until a safer time to open, while some have unfortunately gone under. Uncertainty, anxiety, panic, and stress have spread like wildfire and gripped the hearts of men as the current pandemic overwhelms the nation.

There are job cuts, pay cuts, life cuts due to the present problem. It's a time of faith or fear, a time to lock down and go under, or lock up and look within for innovation. I choose the latter and dream of rising like an eagle amid danger. This is a time for urgency as we can perceive that 'tomorrow' is not promised to us. It is clear in my mind that at such a time as this, it's not enough to just survive. It's a time to repackage and make oneself 'essential' in order to thrive where many have sadly given up hope. This book, birthed in restricted times, is more than just a recipe book. It's a book to inspire you and me, that all hope is not lost as long as we have breath. It's time to find the hero in us. In Shakespeare's book, 'Julius Caesar', Caesar says that, "Cowards die many times before their deaths".

Considering the current events, we must face life like soldiers, like eagles in the battle against the Covid-19 virus. Let's raise our fighting strategy! If death shall come, where will it find us? Hopefully in the place of our calling, doing what we were purposed for. You might have heard the sad story of the eagle that thought it was a chicken and died a chicken, or the inspirational one of another eagle that grew up with chickens and still learned to fly despite its surroundings.

I made a commitment to myself many years ago that my destination was not meant for the pot, but for the top. Chickens end up in the pot, eagles at the top, flying gracefully. If the saying is true that *things happen for you and not to you*, then it's time to seize opportunities, take a leap of faith, and live your dream.

My Story

Every New Year comes with excitement and a new desire for a better life, and so for many people, including me, 2020 would have been a year of double for your trouble, double blessing, 20/20 vision. But it turned out to be a year of despair, pain, worry, bad news, frustration and anxiety around the world. In a nutshell, the year did not come packaged like the expected dream. It took me a couple of months after the first lockdown to realise that 2020 may not have looked like a dream, but what had been handed to us was a precious commodity. We had been given TIME – a gap year to fill with essentials, despite the limitations. The question is what could anyone do with time under lockdown except to listen to the daily nerve-racking media coverage of the Covid-19 pandemic.

Nonetheless, the 'eagle mentality' kicked in a few times fighting with my 'chicken' self, until I finally revisited my home-based catering dream, 'Flair Cookery', which I had abandoned four years earlier. It is in actively engaging myself in the business during the lockdown that I realised the need to upgrade Flair Cookery's status beyond ground level.
It was time to mount up like an eagle. It was at

this stage that I connected with Chikumo via social media and she offered me her services to improve the Flair Cookery brand, which resulted in increased traffic on all business sites. I understood why my husband always encouraged me to be the driver instead of being the passenger if I wanted to develop myself. He explained that experienced drivers were more resilient as they have learned the ability to navigate, even when they see a road sign saying 'closed'. They do not panic because they know from experience that when one lane is shut, another will have opened, because every driver has a vision to complete their journey.

During lockdown, the signs ahead pointed to networking and to taking my business online. It required me to steadily follow the diversion signs. I took the alternative route where I progressed into various projects and made connections that have changed my life. It has been an amazing experience to view life from an eagle's perspective. I learned eagles soar on rising currents and not on 'breaking' news, because they are committed to their vision of a better future self.

"There are no traffic jams on the extra mile" **Zig Ziglar**

It's not easy to step out of our comfort zones or to be motivated in the face of many challenges, and so it's important to sift what we listen to. I love listening to stuff that tickles my ears. I am constantly listening to the inspirational Word and great motivational speakers and coaches like Les Brown, Benjamin Hardy, Dean Graziosi, and many inspiring chefs like Marco Pierre White. I also enjoy seeing progress from influential chefs such as Chris Galvin, who was our executive chef at the Wolseley restaurant café many years ago and has since been running multiple food ventures in London. It is possible!

I am persuaded that for anyone to achieve their dream, not only must they believe that they can, but they should also surround themselves with like-minded people-the power of proximity. They say we become like the people we spend the most time with. It is therefore important to qualify people into our circle by what comes out of their mouths because words have the power to create life or death.

It is also said that 'birds of a feather flock together' and so I 'zoomed' in with positive groups online and networked with people from far and wide who are also in pursuit of their dreams or may have arrived. In the book,

'Personality Isn't Permanent', Benjamin Hardy explains that one's 'future self' is more important than their 'present self' therefore, what we do today is a preparation for our tomorrow. It is therefore pivotal to invest the time available on personal development, whilst polishing up on skills or starting new ventures. It is also of great importance to fly with eagle-minded people, those with vision and purpose, especially in the current times of mental and economic turmoil. Life is a rollercoaster, hence motivating oneself and others is key to a healthy lifestyle.

I cannot express the magnitude of how important it is for us to encourage ourselves daily. We must speak to ourselves with power positive words that awaken our purpose and challenge us to keep moving, and so I say to you, the reader, what I would speak to myself,

"You are the victor, not the victim, the dream and not the dreamer. You are the hope and not the hopeless, the eagle and not the chicken. What if, what is happening in the world, is happening for you and not to you? What would you do with your time?"

It's time to spread your wings and fly. I visited a nursery school some years ago and on the wall was written these words.

'You will never know how far you can fly, until you spread your wings'

To chicken out is to fear taking risks. It is to await the day of being cooked, and that's not a good feeling. I have been challenged to look within and see where I can add value to myself and to others and I hope you will do the same.

With a background in Hospitality and Culinary Arts, I have used the ingredients I know and love to serve you some food for thought. Go for your dream! This book will encourage you on your journey to have a *'Yes I can!'* attitude.

I hope you have realised that my major theme for this book is, 'yes, chic-ken!' Let it be your attitude too. It is possible!

To roast or to be roasted is the choice. This is not time to chicken out but to take on the Prime Minister's challenge to *'build, build, build',* not a nest, but your future self. I am building my 'Chicken Inn' so that I can have my chicken and eat it at the same time!
Wouldn't you? *What ingredients or tools do you have to make a start on your dream?*

What trade or craft have you mastered that can take you to the next level? You can do anything you set your mind to achieve.

I hope this book will serve you well so that not only will you revive your dreams or absorb new ideas, but that you will enjoy the chicken recipes and stories shared in this book. Les Brown says if you want to shift, *"You've gotta be hungry"*. It is my sincere hope that this book will awaken your creativity as you cook your way to success, lick your fingers and the best part will be chewing them bones, because you can-period! All things are possible!

Miss Eagle South Africa 2018 said, "Impossible is a word in the vocabulary of chickens. Eagles see the word 'impossible' as 'I'm possible'". The great book speaks even louder, declaring that
'Nothing shall be impossible to him that believes.'

More than a chicken dream

I will happily eat chicken anytime and any day but when I was growing up, chicken was reserved for special occasions. It was a dish for celebrations – Christmas, birthdays and weddings. I remember when I was in boarding school, parents used to bring chicken for their children on the Visiting/Parents' Day, this was also a special occasion. Chicken on visiting day was extra special- an irresistible, scrumptious treat. It was something most students looked forward to receiving, perhaps more than the visit. You could never mistake the aroma of fried or roasted chicken. It just filled the atmosphere and saturated the dormitory corridors. It's that aromatic smell of soul food that awakens every sense in your body and makes you feel so hungry that you just want to eat.

Unfortunately, I never had the pleasure of getting chicken on this special day as my parents would bring us some of the fine and healthier produce from the farm, which was good, but it was not the same as fried chicken. However, I was still incredibly grateful.

Roasted/grilled/fried chicken was also the dish prepared for visitors in the best serving dishes taken out of the display unit. Another time that chicken was cooked in that method and wrapped in foil was for long trips and journeys and so, to eat chicken, you had better be ***going somewhere***! I am reminiscing over the lingering aroma of the scrumptious chicken reserved for these special occasions. Interestingly, my kids too like to eat chicken on their travel journeys, chicken wraps, chicken tikka and fried chicken.

Amazingly, hunger kicks in right at the beginning of the journey when they begin to ask for food. I guess it's the excitement of travelling or perhaps it shows that we are always hungry on this journey of life, maybe not just for food, but for something to quench our thirst for life or a hunger to fulfill our dreams, which we all experience at different stages of life.

Some people put an urgent demand on their hunger while others wait for a time when the conditions are right. Whatever the case may be, we must either cater for the journey or ensure we stop at a Chicken Inn along the way.

What we cannot create for ourselves, we will need to get from other people and that could be your 'Chicken Inn'. *What profitable services are you able to offer people on this journey?*

I remember as a student in London, having to look after every penny. I did not have extra money to buy takeaways. I was very fortunate that my sister who is an air hostess for a national airline would visit me on her trips and take me to the KFC takeaway across the road from my college every time she came.

My dream for eating chicken on visitor's day was fulfilled many times. It is still very memorable. My desire then moved from, wanting to be given chicken to purchasing it for myself. I used to wonder and ask my sister if I would ever be in a position to buy the fried chicken with my own money. She would laugh and say, "Of course you will", and I did.

Today I care more about frying my own chicken the way I like it and serving others.

Chicken - a healthy choice

Chicken has always been seen as a healthier option to red meat. It's low in saturated fat and high in protein. It has essential minerals and vitamins that help to build muscles and keep the heart and body healthy. The chicken breast is the most lean and tender part of chicken and therefore needs less cooking time to keep it moist and juicy. Chicken is a versatile ingredient which can be flavoured and cooked in many ways as seen in this book. Every part of the chicken can be used to make healthy, tasty dishes, with healthier alternative cooking methods such as poaching.

Instead of throwing away bones, it is a great idea to make white or brown stock to use for soups and stews especially in cold seasons. Stock is extraordinarily rich in flavour hence, it is used as a base for making many classic sauces. It can also be used to braise rice and to season a variety of dishes. Stock will freeze well in freezer bags or plastic containers for up to 3 to 4 months.

Equipment for preparing, storing and cooking chicken

Only the basic tools are required to start a catering business, or to cook the recipes in this book for your friends and families at home. It's important however, to follow food safety and hygiene requirements for use and storage of equipment such as cleaning and using colour-coded boards to avoid cross contamination.

Knives

There's an ancient proverb that says a sharp knife is a chef's best friend. We all need friends like that, who will cut to the chase and not waste our precious time and money, friends that give cutting and constructive advice.

Colour-coded chopping boards

Keep it practical, use red boards for raw meat and yellow boards for cooked meat to avoid cross contamination.

Metal colander

Multi-use equipment is of great value. Use a colander to wash vegetables and herbs. Additionally, it can be used to create a steamer.

Plastic or stainless-steel bowls

'No glass' rules are used for food preparation, especially if cooking with children to avoid accidents through breakages. Use the bowls for mixing or marinating ingredients.

Spice grinder

Every kitchen needs one. It's a game changer for crushing whole spices and making your own spice mixtures.

Blender

Great for reducing chopping time. Perfect for mixing marinades. If you don't have one, you can finely chop the ingredients required.

Sieve

Use a metal one or a conical strainer so it can sit nicely on the pot. It is necessary for separating the good from the bad and the needed from the unwanted. Great for straining/passing sauces.

Pots of different sizes

You will need at least two pots, medium and large depending on the number of people you are catering for. The recipes in this book will feed five or more people per recipe.

Measuring spoons

Use measuring spoons to weigh out the spices or measure with a teaspoon. When more experienced, you can use the eye to judge the amount of spice required.

Freezer bags, cling film, greaseproof paper, foil, plastic containers with lids

These are all essential aids for covering and storing marinated chicken.
Use a combination of greaseproof and foil paper to cover the chicken when cooking. For freezing, use the freezer bags and plastic containers.

Griddle pan

A griddle pan is a flat pan that contributes to healthier cooking methods as less oil is used in the cooking process. Griddling also impacts on the texture and flavour of the chicken. The griddle lines add an appetising and appealing finish to the cooked chicken. See the picture of the chicken dish on the front cover of this cookbook.

Frying pan

A good non-stick wide pan is essential for frying food. It's important to fry a few pieces of chicken at a time to brown the chicken and seal in the juices. Too much meat in a frying pan can result to lack of colour on the chicken and a shift in the cooking method. (See different cookery methods explained in this book).

Deep fryer

This is necessary but not essential, as a good deep pot can do the job. Ensure safety measures are in place when deep frying in pots, such as never leaving oil to heat up without supervision.

Roasting tins

Keep at least two different sizes, medium and large, to allow the even spread of the chicken. The amount of chicken in a tray and the size of the tin can affect the cooking time.

Mallet/rolling pin

Either of the tools can be used to bash chicken to make escalopes, (thinned down meat). The finished product is worth the work, as it takes less time to cook. Bashing the chicken can be a great stress reliever.

Blue plastic disposable gloves

When preparing and mixing ingredients such as chillies and turmeric, its best to use gloves. Wearing gloves in the preparation of food also helps to keep food safe and protect customers from food poisoning. It is important to change gloves and to wash hands when mixing different marinades or touching raw to cooked food.

Essential dry store ingredients:

Oils

Olive, rapeseed, coconut, and sunflower are my favourite oils. I use the oils for cooking, baking, making dressings, marinades, and infused oils such as chilli, sesame, roast garlic, and herb. The oils are used for either flavouring dishes or for gifting others. Making your own flavour oils is both economical and of great value. Extra Virgin Olive oil must not be used for deep fat frying as it is expensive and has a low smoking point. It is best used for dressings or drizzling on food.

Spices

I tend to buy whole spices in small bottles to preserve the quality of the spices. I also enjoy tempering and blending my own spice mixes which makes marinating easier as the fresh, homemade seasonings are readily available. I always store black pepper, white pepper, table salt, sea salt, cinnamon, cloves, star anise, allspice, turmeric, cumin, coriander, a variety of crushed chillies, cayenne, fennel seeds, mustard seeds, mace, and nutmeg. Store and blend your favourite spices. Be creative! I personally avoid buying ready-made seasonings like chicken seasoning as I prefer homemade.

Dried herbs

I do not store too many dried herbs as I also prefer to pick fresh herbs from the garden. However, I keep dried thyme and oregano in the cupboard. For making curries I store methi leaves that should be soaked in hot water and drained before using. Remember this tip when making the Butter chicken recipe.

Think about your favourite herbs to grow in the garden or on windowsills. Some of the easy herbs to grow are chives, curly parsley, bay leaf, mint and rosemary.

Other dry store essentials

Coconut milk, tinned tomatoes, tomato puree, sundried tomatoes, olives, a variety of beans - dried and tinned, chickpeas, lentils, flour, honey, sesame seeds, peanut butter, vinegar, corn flour, soy, mustard, rice, and pasta are a must have.

Preparation is key to success in life.

'Mise en place' is the culinary term for the preparation of ingredients and dishes prior to service, in any successful kitchen. A lack of preparation can result to, disaster, panic, and complaints.

Preparation gives us the ability to adjust when situations go wrong. What is the alternative? What can I do best to control or fix the situation? How can I solve the problem? Having worked in many fast-paced restaurants, I have learned the importance of preparation and organisation to enable me to think on my feet. If you fail to 'mise en place', not only will you experience pressure and anxiety in work, but you would not survive the heat and fury of the Head Chef, on top of the pressures of working in a hot kitchen.

'Mise en place'- everything in its place is the answer for calming nerves and for increased productivity in any business. It's so much easier to see any shortages and manage problems where there is a flow. In the same way, take stock of your life on a daily, weekly, monthly basis, depending on what you want to achieve. Identifying problematic issues in time will save you from many troubles. Being on top of your

game gives the advantage of a bird's-eye view.

Whatever your situation, there is always hope for a better life when we begin to self-examine ourselves. Every day we are faced with change and new challenges and thus we must adapt and prepare for success. We are living in a time for no excuses! Take preparatory steps for a better future and refuse to be a battery chicken hanging on for dear life! Take charge of your station, put it in some order and if you find that you are lacking in ingredients, get creative and find alternatives, or get what is required. Reach out for support. Do something! Take the challenge but refuse to chicken out.

Research has shown that more than 90% of chickens in the UK are raised in crowded broiler sheds with not enough room to move around freely. Some of these chickens don't survive long enough to be slaughtered and enjoyed for special occasions. Unless we want to find ourselves in these unpleasant circumstances, I suggest we go 'organic', 'free range', take flying lessons, but by no means should we remain stuck, lacking a 'future self' plan. Our unwillingness to face the task of preparation and personal development can become a hurdle to our success and land us in dire straits. It's time to move from our seemingly comfortable places which do not provide any benefits and fly with the eagles.

Preparing poultry

We eat with our eyes first, so presentation is key. Depending on where you live or shop, you might get your chicken from the local butchery, supermarket or from your own back yard, hence, preparation of the chicken will differ. However, the end result must be clean, without feathers and wiped dry before cooking. Research has shown that most chicken sold in the UK carries campylobacter bacteria which causes food poisoning so it is not advisable to wash the chicken, otherwise bacteria will transfer in all directions, via the water droplets to surfaces, equipment and hands.

However, many home cooks prefer to wash chicken in a lemon and vinegar solution but the advice from health experts is to wipe the chicken with a disposable cloth rather than washing it. It is especially important after preparation of raw meats to wash hands.

Chicken must be thoroughly cooked to 75 degrees or above to kill bacteria. If no temperature probe is available, a small cut can be made through the thicker part of the chicken to see if the juices are clear, and the texture of the chicken is no longer tough. If the juices are pink and the chicken is still tough when pressed, continue cooking the chicken otherwise there might be a risk of food poisoning.

Marinating/seasoning

This is necessary to add flavour to the chicken. Some dishes call for marinating at least 24 hours in advance to maximise the flavour and tenderise the chicken. However, if time is not permitting, half an hour will be sufficient.

To season chicken, it's best to make homemade marinades as shown in our recipes. Be creative with the ingredients in your cupboard or pantry, you will be surprised at what you can achieve. Many people have their store cupboard full, with a variety of spices they never use, almost like *shelved dreams*.

When it comes to herbs, it's a great idea to grow your own as well as garlic and chillies as it's more economical and a fun activity for the family. However, use as many of the ingredients you already have before buying more. Never be limited by a recipe but certainly, learn from it.

Always think creativity, health eating, budget and flavour.

Cutting

Chicken can be cooked whole or cut into pieces. Cut the chicken to suit the style of cooking, for example spatchcock for grilling. Also consider the number of people you want to feed or the cooking time you have available. The important thing is to use a sharp knife when cutting chicken.

It can be cheaper to cut a whole chicken than to purchase precut pieces. However, if wanting to buy a preferred cut such as drumsticks only or thighs, wings, breasts, its best to buy precut to avoid wastage.

Wastage

Waste not want not! If preparing whole chickens reserve the feet, gizzards, necks, and livers for other dishes such as liver pate. Any leftovers or unwanted ingredients can be added to your compost for nourishing your veggie patch.

Storing and recycling

Raw chicken must always be stored in sealed containers and covered with clingfilm and stored at the bottom of the fridge to avoid cross-contamination. Any leftover cooked chicken can be chilled quickly, cling filmed and labelled before storing in the fridge for a maximum of three to four days. It should also be thoroughly reheated **once** to avoid food poisoning.

It is a great idea to be creative with the menu. Transform any leftover chicken into hot or cold 'new' dishes. Make sandwich fillings with leftover chicken breast and add pesto (see our recipe) or add any of your favourite toppings or spread. You could also transform leftover chicken cooked on a Wednesday e.g., roasted chicken to Friday's curry, bulked up with pulses and vegetables.

Chicken can also be preserved by freezing it raw or cooked. It is good practice to label any food that is put in the fridge or freezer, especially with our busy lifestyles. Label the name of the dish, allergens, when it was cooked, refrigerated or frozen to avoid food poisoning. It is crucial to fully thaw chicken in the fridge before cooking or reheating.

More than one way to cook a chicken

Chicken is on our menu two or three times a week due to family and customer demand. Adding seasoning to your chicken will ensure that it is full of flavour. There are various ways of cooking chicken as shown in the cookbook. Cooking methods impact on texture, colour, flavour and bring variety to the menu.

Grilling

This is when prepared food is cooked by radiated heat on contact grills, salamanders or barbecue units. The chicken is brushed with oil or marinade and placed on the grill, turning with tongs to allow an even cook.

Frying

Frying can either be shallow or deep fried. Food is cooked in a preheated pan with a small amount of oil or in a deep fat fryer with loads of preheated oil. It is especially important that the oil is sizzling hot otherwise the chicken will absorb too much oil. To drain the fat off the chicken, place the chicken on kitchen paper and then on a high rack which sits in an oven tray. More oil will drip onto the tray whilst the chicken is cooking or keeping warm in the oven until its ready to be served.

Roasting

Roasting can be done on a rotisserie or in the oven. This is a dry heat cooking method which requires fat to brown the meat and to keep it moist. *Pot roasting* differs from roasting in that the chicken is first covered in the initial cooking process. The lid or foil is then removed to finish off the roasting.

Baking

It is the process of cooking food, by dry heat in a pre-heated oven. In this book I have interchanged the word roasting and baking as they are often used to mean the same thing when discussing cooking chicken. However, in baking the chicken is often covered.

Steaming

Steaming is cooking food with water vapour which is the steam. If you haven't got a steamer, another way to steam is to put boiling water in a pan and sit a metal colander. Cover the bottom of the colander with excess foil then greaseproof paper. Place your seasoned or marinated chicken in the prepared steamer then cover with a greaseproof paper and bring the excess foil over the top to tightly secure the chicken like a parcel. The steam will cook the chicken until its tender. This is a great method for cooking chicken breast, and a healthier option as no oil is required in the cooking process.

Griddling

Griddling involves cooking food on a lightly oiled metal plate which is one of my favourite ways for cooking chicken. (see griddle pan for more information)

Stir fry

It is the quick frying of food in a frying pan with fat e.g., oil. You can stir fry chicken fajitas on a griddle pan, frying pan or a wok.

Poaching

Poaching can be deep or shallow - partly covered. The food is immersed in boiling cooking liquor such as stock and cooked gently on temperatures below boiling point.

Braising

Chicken is cooked in the oven with minimum liquid and covered with a lid. To start off the cooking process, the chicken is browned by frying or sweating which means gentle frying with little oil and covered with a lid to stop from colouring.

Stewing

It is the slow cooking of cut pieces of prepared food in minimum liquid e.g., fricassees. Both the liquid and the food (vegetables and chicken) when cooked make the stew and are always served together.

Boiling

Boiling is cooking seasoned chicken in a pot with liquid and covered with a lid. The liquid is brought to a boil then reduced to a simmer to finish the cooking.

Kitchen tips

- Keep it simple, do not stress.
- Use alternative ingredients if necessary.
- 'Mise en place' is key.
- Make your spice blends and marinades in advance and store them in bottles until needed or gift others.
- Plan your dishes in advance.
- Create your weekly menus.
- Season your chicken with salt and pepper.
- Taste your food for flavour & add your flair.
- Clean as you go.

Use the notes pages at the back of this cookbook to plan your dishes and write your alternative ingredients.

My favourite inspirational quotes

This is how I like my chicken, sizzling, scrummy and seasoned all the way.
Portia Ruzario

A recipe has no soul. You as the cook, must bring soul to the recipe.
Thomas Keller

Cookery is not chemistry. It is an art. It requires instinct and taste rather than exact measurements.
Marcel Boulestin

One of the greatest pleasures of my life has been that I have never stopped learning about good cooking and good food.
Edna Lewis

You've gotta be hungry.
Les Brown

Healthy eating is cooking and enjoying homecooked food that has been seasoned with love.
Portia Ruzario

Recipes

- Ginger, honey & soy chicken
- Pesto chicken
- Parmesan chicken
- Grilled spatchcock chicken
- Fried chicken
- Roast chicken 1.6 – 1.8 kg
- Sunshine chicken
- Salt and pepper chicken
- Jerk style chicken
- Chicken curry – flavours of Bahia
- Braised red pepper and tomato chicken
- Lemon & herb chicken
- BBQ chicken
- Malay chicken curry
- Peri Peri chicken
- Cajun chicken
- Harissa chicken
- Butter chicken curry (makhani)
- Warm chicken and orzo salad
- Chicken tikka
- Chicken Yassa
- Chipotle chicken
- Chicken fajitas
- Pot roast chicken
- White chicken casserole

Examples of chicken menus

Combine 2/3 of our chicken dishes onto your weekly menu. Make sauces from our base recipes and marinades. Add plenty of vegetables and carbohydrates to your chicken dish. Here are examples of finished menus.

Weekly Menu

M — PERI PERI CHICKEN, BAKED CHIPS AND CHAKALAKA

T — MALAY CHICKEN WITH LENTILS AND PILAU RICE

W — FRIED CHICKEN, MAC 'N' CHEESE WITH CRISPY SALAD

T — JERK CHICKEN, PLANTAIN AND JOLLOF RICE

F — BUTTER CHICKEN CURRY WITH CUMIN RICE AND CUCUMBER SALAD

S — ROAST CHICKEN WITH ROAST POTATOES AND STEAMED VEG

Base Recipes

CHICKEN STOCK (Makes 2-4 liters)

Ingredients

3 chicken carcass or bones
1 large onion
1 leek
2 medium carrots
2 celery stalks
Fresh thyme
Fresh parsley stalks
2 bay leaves
1 tbsp peppercorns

Directions

1. Roast chicken bones till golden brown in the oven at 200C. Turn the bones in between cooking.

2. In a large pan fry off mirepoix which is your diced veg until its browned.

3. Remove bones from the oven (should be browned on both sides).

4. Place the bones in a pan with the vegetables

and cover with cold water. You want just enough water to cover the bones.

5. Add a handful of herbs; thyme, parsley stalks, 2 bay leaves

and a tablespoon of peppercorns.

6. Bring to the boil and remove the debris that forms at the top using a ladle.

7. Reduce to a simmer and keep removing the debris as it comes up in a foam. This will take 2-3 hours for the stock to be concentrated.

8. Once you have a nice golden colour stock, pass/strain the stock through a sieve and reserve it. *Place your chilled waste vegetables in a compost.*

9. Chill the stock. After chilling, remove any fat or debris from the top of the stock with a spoon then freeze in small containers until ready to use.

TOMATO & RED PEPPER SAUCE – WEST AFRICAN STYLE

Ingredients

2 large onions, roughly chopped
3 large red peppers, deseeded diced
5 garlic cloves, peeled
50g ginger peeled and chopped
10g scotch bonnet
500g tin of tomatoes
300g tomato puree
2 tbsp curry powder
5 tbsp sunflower oil
2L chicken stock
1 tbsp thyme
1 bay leaf fresh

Directions

1. Boil the peppers and onions till they become soft and drain the water.

2. Blend the onions, peppers, garlic, ginger, scotch bonnet, tinned tomatoes, and tomato puree until smooth.

3. In a large pan add oil and heat on a medium heat.

4. Add the curry powder and fry for about 2 mins then add the blended veg. Cook for ½ an hour occasionally stirring the sauce so that it doesn't stick or burn.

5. Add the chicken stock and herbs then simmer till the stock is reduced for another ½ an hour.

6. Stir the sauce. Allow to simmer for about 10 more minutes and taste for seasoning. The sauce should be smooth, spicy, and tasty. Adjust seasoning with more spice if required.

Use the sauce to braise chicken, cook rice and mix into curries or your favourite stews. It can be frozen for 3/4 months.

GINGER, HONEY AND SOY CHICKEN

Ingredients

1 kg chicken thighs (breasts can be used as well
and require less cooking)
3 tablespoons stem ginger, finely chopped
2 tablespoons honey
2 tablespoons soy sauce
1 teaspoon chilli flakes
Juice of lime
1 shallot
2 garlic cloves
Salt & pepper

Directions

1. Blitz all of the ingredients (except the chicken) in a blender to a smooth paste.

2. In a bowl, mix the chicken with the spice marinade and a little salt and pepper by hand until all the chicken is coated. Leave in the fridge to marinate overnight.

3. Preheat the oven to 150C.

4. Place the chicken in an oven proof dish and bake for 30- 40 minutes or until cooked through.

5. Once cooked, turn the oven up to 180C and cook for a further 15 minutes or until the chicken is sticky and has a lovely charred colour to it.

Garnish with lime, red chilli, and spring onions.

PESTO CHICKEN

Ingredients

1kg chicken drumsticks
50g pine nuts
50g grated parmesan cheese.
150g fresh basil, washed and dried
200ml olive oil
2 garlic cloves

Directions

1. Lightly toast the pine nuts.

2. Blitz the pine nuts, cheese, basil, and garlic in a blender. Slowly add the oil to the mixture till its blended and coarse with a vibrant green colour. Taste for seasoning and store in a jar, in the fridge.

3. Lightly season the chicken with salt and pepper.

4. Marinade chicken with 5-7 tablespoons of pesto. Keep the marinated chicken in the fridge overnight.

5. Roast at 180C in the oven for 45 minutes. Increase temperature to 200C for more colour for another 15 minutes or until cooked.

Store the remaining pesto in the fridge and use for pasta salads, cheese sandwiches, burgers, sundried tomato and mozzarella, tomato and pesto canapes.

PARMESAN CHICKEN

Ingredients

500g chicken breast, cut in half (butterfly)
300g plain flour
5 eggs, beaten
*200g panko breadcrumbs
50g parmesan cheese, grated
Salt and pepper, to taste
1 tbsp chopped parsley (optional)
*If you do not have panko breadcrumbs, blend
some bread crusts

Directions

1. Place the chicken one at a time inside a thick freezer bag and bash with a mallet.

2. Take 3 bowls. In one bowl add the plain flour and season with salt and pepper. In the second bowl, add the eggs and in the third bowl, add the breadcrumbs mixed with the grated parmesan cheese and a tablespoon of chopped parsley (optional).

3. Dip the chicken into the flour and shake off any excess.

4. Dip the same piece of chicken into the beaten egg then into the breadcrumb mix. Repeat the process until all the chicken has been coated.

5. Add enough oil in a pan to shallow fry the chicken on a medium heat. When the oil is hot fry the chicken 4/5 minutes on each side. If not fully cooked, finish the cooking in the oven.

Serve the chicken with salad on a toasted bun topped with garlic mayonnaise and a side of chips.
*We have topped the chicken with the remaining pesto from the previous dish.

THAI FLAVOURED GRILLED SPATCHCOCK CHICKEN

Ingredients

1 Whole chicken
30g fresh coriander (include stem), chopped
5g kaffir leaves (fresh or frozen)
10 fresh bird's eye green chillies
4 shallots, diced
4 garlic cloves, crushed
2 tbsp toasted coriander seeds
1 tsp cracked black pepper
5ml dark soy sauce
50g palm sugar or soft brown sugar
3 tablespoons olive oil
Juice from 2 limes

Directions

1. To spatchcock chicken, place chicken on a board and remove the backbone with some scissors. Reserve the bone for stock or for another dish. Turn the chicken with the breast up and press down the chicken until it's flat.

2. Blend all the ingredients except chicken and lime. Cook the marinade for about 20 mins then add a squeeze of the lime juice. Add a bit more olive oil and seasoning if required. The marinade must be sweet, spicy, salty and citrusy to taste.

3. Steam seasoned chicken for 30mins/ boil for 20 mins.

4. Brush chicken with marinade.

5. Place under the grill on medium heat and continue to baste or brush with marinade for 20-25 mins or until chicken is cooked.

FRIED CHICKEN

Ingredients

1 whole chicken/ chicken pieces seasoned
2 teaspoons cayenne pepper
2 tsp paprika
1 tsp garlic powder
2 tsp onion powder
½ tsp dried oregano
½ tsp basil
½ tsp thyme
1 tsp chilli flakes
Juice from ½ lemon
300ml buttermilk
200g self-raising flour
100g corn flour
1 egg, beaten

Directions

1. Cut a whole chicken into pieces.

2. In a bowl, season the chicken with lemon, salt, pepper, cayenne pepper, chilli flakes, paprika, garlic powder oregano, basil, thyme, onion powder and 300ml buttermilk. Leave to marinate overnight in the fridge.

3. Remove chicken from the fridge, mix in the beaten egg and place to one side.

4. In a separate bowl, mix the self-raising flour, corn flour, salt and pepper to taste.

5. Coat each piece of chicken in the flour mix, shaking off the surplus.

6. Deep fry in pre-heated hot oil 170C, frying 3/4 pieces at a time in a wide pot or deep fat fryer for 12 - 15 minutes or until golden brown. If using a probe, the chicken should be 75 degrees or above.

7. Place chicken on a tray with kitchen paper to drain the fat. *See notes on frying*.

ROAST CHICKEN 1.6KG – 1.8KG

Ingredients

1 whole chicken
1 carrot, medium, peeled
½ of a whole garlic head, including peels
½ onion
4 sprigs parsley
6 sprigs thyme
1 bay leaf
½ lemon
4 tbsp oil
1 tbsp butter
Salt and pepper to taste

Directions

1. Season the chicken with salt & pepper. Place all the ingredients (except the oil and butter) in the cavity of the chicken.

2. Rub the chicken with butter and oil.

3. Roast in an oven proof dish at 200C for 90 minutes or until cooked

4. Rest the chicken before carving. Use the flavoured juices from the chicken to make gravy thickened with a little corn flour paste and cooked through. Taste for seasoning.

 Serve with roast potatoes and vegetables of your choice.

SUNSHINE CHICKEN

Ingredients

1kg chicken, thighs & drumsticks
2 tbsp Jamaican curry powder
½ tsp cumin seeds, toasted
½ tsp fennel seeds, toasted
½ tsp ground allspice
½ tsp garlic powder
¼ small scotch bonnet
3 tsp chilli flakes
1 tbsp fresh thyme
12 pimento seeds
1 tin coconut milk
½ squeeze lime juice
Salt and pepper
3 mixed peppers cut into strips
½ bunch of spring onions sliced at an angle

Directions

1. Mix all the ingredients (except the spring onions and mixed peppers) in a bowl and leave to marinate in the fridge for 3 hours or overnight.

2. Place in an oven proof dish and bake at 180C covered with foil for 1 hour, turning the chicken after the first 30 mins.

3. Remove foil to let the chicken brown on both sides about 20 minutes before adding the peppers and spring onions. Taste for seasoning.

Serve with grilled sweet potatoes or rice and peas

SALT & PEPPER CHICKEN

Ingredients

500g diced chicken breast/wings
½ tsp onion powder
½ tsp ginger powder
½ tsp Chinese 5 spice
1 tsp soy sauce
110g corn flour
1 egg
1 tbsp water
1 tsp cayenne pepper
3 spring onions, sliced
½ red onion, sliced
1 red chilli, diced
Salt & cracked black pepper

Directions

1. In a bowl, add the chicken, onion powder, ginger powder, Chinese spice, soy sauce, 10g corn flour, cayenne pepper, egg, water, salt, and pepper and mix.

2. Leave to marinate for at least 3 hours in the fridge.

3. In a separate bowl, add the remaining corn flour with salt and pepper.

4. Dip the chicken in corn flour and shake. Repeat procedure till the chicken has been coated in the corn flour mix.

5. Deep fry a few pieces of chicken at a time at 170C using a deep fryer or Dutch pot (1-2 liters oil should suffice depending on the size of the pot). Seal the chicken and then lift chicken out of the fryer.

6. Increase the temperature to 180C put back the chicken to fry until it reaches a golden colour. If using a deep pan, increase the heat.

7. In another pan using a little oil from the deep fryer, fry the spring onions, red onion, and chilli until soft.

8. Toss the crispy chicken in the fried vegetable.

9. Add more pepper and salt if required and serve with oven baked chips and crispy salad.

JERK STYLE CHICKEN

Ingredients

2kg chicken, on the bone
1 bunch of spring onions, sliced
20g scotch bonnet, diced
5 tsp allspice
5 tbsp cider vinegar
5 tbsp soy sauce
5 tbsp soft brown sugar
5 garlic cloves
3 shallots chopped
3 tsp cinnamon powder
1 tbsp dried thyme
50g peeled ginger
Juice of 2 limes
Salt & pepper
Garnish-spring onions, red onion and lime wedges

Directions

1. Blend all the ingredients (except the chicken) until a smooth paste forms and place in a bottle with a lid. This can be kept up to 4 weeks in the fridge.

2. Take 7-8 tablespoons of the marinade and mix into the seasoned chicken, allowing to marinate in the fridge overnight or up to 3 days for maximum flavour.

3. Lay the chicken flat on a tray and place in a preheated oven at 160C and roast for an hour.

4. Increase the temperature to 200C turning and basting the chicken with its juice until charred for another 30 mins or until cooked on the inside.

Serve topped with spring onions, red onions and lime wedges and enjoy with a bowl of rice and peas.

CHICKEN CURRY – FLAVOURS OF BAHIA

Ingredients

1kg chicken pieces, thigh or leg
Juice of 1 lime
1tsp coriander
2 tsp cumin
2 tsp turmeric
1 tsp garlic powder
1 thumb size fresh ginger, diced/finely grated
5g Scotch bonnet pepper
1 tsp chilli powder
1 tin coconut milk
1 tsp flaked chilli
1 tbsp soft brown sugar
1 hand full fresh coriander
1 hand full fresh parsley
Salt & pepper

Directions

1. Blitz all the ingredients (except the chicken) and cover the chicken with the marinade. Leave to marinade over night.

2. Preheat the oven at 180C.

3. Place the chicken on an oven tray, cover with foil and braise for an hour.

4. Once cooked, remove the foil.

5. Add 6 tbsp of the tomato and pepper sauce (please see tomato & red pepper sauce – West African style recipe).

6. Increase the oven temperature to 200C and bake for 15-20 mins or until browned. Cooking time sometimes depends on the size of the chicken and the oven.

Serve the chicken in its sauce and as an option, bulk up with cooked black beans.

Garnish with fresh coriander and serve with Brazilian rice.

BRAISED RED PEPPER & TOMATO CHICKEN

Ingredients

2kg chicken, thigh and drumsticks
1 litre of tomato and red pepper sauce – West African style (see tomato and red pepper sauce in base recipes)
2 red onions, diced
2 red peppers, diced
Salt & pepper to taste

Directions

1. Pan fry the seasoned chicken for 5-10 minutes or until it's a golden colour.

2. Place the red pepper and tomato sauce in an oven tray and place chicken on top and mix. Cover with foil and bake at 180C for 1.5 hours.

3. Remove the foil and place the chicken back in the oven and cook till browned.

4. In another pan, fry the onions and peppers. Add to the chicken and serve with rice.

Taste and add more chilli, salt and pepper if required.

LEMON & HERB CHICKEN

Ingredients

20 pieces of chicken, drumsticks and thighs
2 lemons, juiced, de-seeded and cut into wedges
1 tsp bird's eye chilli flakes
1 bay leaf
1tsp honey
1 tsp garlic powder
1 tsp dried thyme
1 tsp dried oregano
Handful of fresh herbs mixed together (rosemary, chives, parsley, oregano)
Salt and pepper to taste

Directions

1. Mix the chicken with the lemon rind and its juice and all the other ingredients. Leave to marinate overnight.

2. Grill the chicken at 180C for 1-1.5 hours or until cooked through, turning occasionally with tongs

Serve with sweet potato wedges and a mixed leaf salad.

BBQ CHICKEN

Ingredients

2kg chicken, drumsticks and thighs
2 tsp fennel seeds toasted
2 tbsp smoked paprika
1 tbsp garlic powder
3 tbsp cider vinegar
3 tbsp soft brown sugar
1 tbsp crushed chilli flakes
½ tbsp ginger powder
6 tbsp ketchup
2 bay leaves
Thumb size sliced ginger
2 tbsp soy sauce
2 tbsp Worcestershire sauce
Salt and pepper

Directions

1. In a bowl, mix all of the ingredients together. Leave to marinate in the fridge overnight.

2. Pre-heat the oven at 180C.

3. Roast for 1 hour and 20 minutes or until chicken is sticky, golden and cooked through.

Serve with chips or roast potatoes and salad.

MALAY CHICKEN CURRY

Ingredients

1 whole chicken, cut into pieces
5 cardamom pods
2 tsp coriander
2 tsp cumin
2 tsp chilli flakes
2 tsp turmeric
1 tsp cinnamon
1 thumb sized portion of ginger, sliced
2 medium size onions, sliced
5 garlic cloves, crushed
2 ripe tomatoes diced
Salt & pepper

Directions

1. Season the chicken before frying in a pan until browned. No oil is required in a nonstick pan as the chicken will release its own fat.

2. Once browned, add all the spices to the chicken and stir for 5 mins.

3. Add the onion, garlic, ginger and stir. Cook for approximately 3 minutes before adding the tomatoes. Next add a little water if there is not enough liquid to make the sauce.

4. Occasionally stir for 20-30 minutes or until the sauce thickens and the chicken is cooked.

Garnish the chicken with fresh coriander. Serve with yellow and white rice.

PERI PERI CHICKEN

Ingredients

25 pieces of chicken, thighs and drumsticks
2 tsp smoked paprika
2 tsp oregano
1 tsp garlic powder
2 tsp onion powder
2 tsp cayenne pepper
1tsp dried coriander
3tsp dried bird's eye chilli flakes
1 lemon, juiced
1 tin coconut milk
Salt and pepper

Directions

1. Place the chicken and spices in a large pot and par boil on a medium heat for 30 minutes.

2. Remove the chicken from remaining marinade and place on a hot oiled griddle pan or place under the grill.

3. Slow cook on a low heat for 15 mins or until the chicken is golden in colour and cooked through whilst continuously basting with the marinade.

4. Turn the chicken and repeat the process for 15 to 30 minutes or until cooked. Keep cooking the sauce till it thickens to serve with the chicken. Serve also with a side of baked chips and salad.

CAJUN CHICKEN

Ingredients

2kg chicken breast
2 tbsp garlic powder
2 tbsp smoked paprika
1 tbsp cayenne pepper
1 tsp chilli flakes
2 tbsp onion powder
1 tbsp dried thyme
1 tbsp dried oregano
3 tbsp olive oil
Salt & pepper

Directions

1. In a bowl, add the chicken and spices. Leave to marinate in the
fridge for 30 minutes or overnight.

2. Preheat the oven at 180C.

3. Roast the chicken for 20 minutes or until cooked through and golden in colour.

Serve on ciabatta bread with garlic mayonnaise and salad.

HARISSA CHICKEN

Ingredients

2kg chicken thighs and drumsticks
4 garlic cloves, peeled
2 tbsp toasted coriander seeds
4 tsp toasted cumin seeds
2 tsp toasted caraway seeds
2 tsp smoked paprika
1 tbsp dried bird's eye chilli soaked in boiling water and drained
10 tbsp olive oil
2 red peppers, sliced
2 red onions, sliced
Salt and pepper, to taste
Coriander (optional)

Directions

1. Blend all the ingredients, excluding the chicken, peppers and onions, until a paste is formed.

2. In a bowl, marinate the chicken with the blended paste and leave
overnight in the fridge.

3. Pre-heat the oven at 180C.

4. Roast the chicken for an hour.

5. Add the peppers and onions.

6. Place back in the oven for another 20 to 30 minutes or until the chicken is thoroughly cooked.

Garnish with coriander and serve with rice or couscous.

BUTTER CHICKEN CURRY (MAKHANI)

Ingredients

800g boneless and skinless thigh chicken
1 garlic clove, peeled and finely chopped
Thumb size ginger, peeled and finely chopped
1 tsp hot chilli powder- Deggi Mirch
2 tbsp lemon juice
100ml Greek yoghurt
1 tsp ground turmeric
1 ½ tsp cumin
1 tsp garam masala
30g fresh coriander
Salt & pepper

For the sauce

2 tbsp sunflower oil
1 onion, diced
1 tsp ground turmeric
1 tsp cumin powder
1 tsp hot chilli powder
200g tomato puree
1 tbsp lemon juice
100g butter
300ml double cream
1 tbsp methi leaves
3 tbsp sugar
Garnish- fresh coriander

Directions

1. Blend the ingredients, excluding the chicken, add the marinate spices in a bowl and mix thoroughly.

2. Add and mix the blended marinade to the seasoned chicken (with salt and pepper). Leave to marinate for half an hour or overnight.

3. Roast in the oven at 180C for 30-45 minutes or until cooked, turning halfway through the cooking.

4. **To make the sauce**, add the oil in a pan and heat gently. Add the turmeric, chilli and cumin. Cook for a few minutes then add the onion and continue stirring.

5. Once the onions are soft, add the tomato puree. Cook for a further 10 minutes and then blend the sauce.

6. Add the cream, lemon juice and methi leaves and keep stirring for 5-10 minutes. Add the butter and sugar and stir.

7. Remove chicken from the oven and add it to the sauce and stir. Taste and adjust seasoning. Garnish with fresh coriander. Serve with rice, flat breads, and cucumber salad.

WARM CHICKEN & ORZO SALAD

Ingredients

2 chicken breasts
1 red pepper, deseeded and thinly sliced
1 red onion, thinly sliced
150g orzo (pasta)
1 tbsp fresh basil
1 tbsp fresh oregano
Pinch dried chilli flakes
1 garlic clove, crushed
50g sundried tomatoes
25g rocket salad
½ tbsp balsamic vinegar
2 tbsp olive oil
Diced feta cheese (optional)

Directions

1. Put the chicken breasts between 2 sheets of cling film and bash flat with a mallet or rolling pin.

2. Heat the oven to 180C. Mix the pepper and onion with 1 tablespoon of oil in an oven proof dish and roast till cooked.

3. Mix the remaining oil, herbs, chilli and garlic then rub over the chicken.

4. Heat a griddle pan and cook the chicken for 4 mins on each side.

5. Cook the pasta following the pack instructions. Drain and set aside in a bowl.

6. Slice the cooked chicken on a yellow board, scrape into the pasta with any juices plus the roasted onion and pepper, sundried tomatoes, rocket, vinegar, diced feta and seasoning.

7. Toss together and eat warm or cold.

CHICKEN TIKKA

Ingredients

4kg chicken of thighs and legs
Juice from 4 lemons
10 garlic cloves
1 thumb sized portion of ginger, peeled and
chopped
30g fresh coriander
500g Greek yogurt
3tsp masala spice
3tsp hot chilli powder
1tsp cinnamon
2tsp cumin powder
2tbsp paprika
3 small red onions, sliced
2 fresh green chillies, sliced
2 yellow peppers, sliced

Directions

1. Excluding the chicken, onion, chilli and peppers, blend all of the ingredients and mix with the chicken in a bowl. Leave to marinate overnight.

2. Roast chicken at 180C for 1.5 hours or until cooked through and browned, turning the chicken halfway through the cooking.

3. Once the chicken is cooked, add the onions, chillies and yellow peppers.

4. Roast for a further 15 to 20 minutes on 200 degrees.

Serve with rice or flatbread or pull the chicken off the bones and use for making sandwiches or wraps.

CHICKEN YASSA

Ingredients

2kg chicken pieces, thighs and legs
165g green pitted olives
2 tbsp whole grain mustard
or any other types of mustard you may have in
your cupboard, e.g., French mustard.
Zest and juice of 4 lemons
5g Scotch bonnet chillies or 2 red bird's eye chillies
cut in half
5 large onions, sliced
1 bay leaf
Salt and pepper
Olive oil

Directions

1. For the marinade, mix all of the ingredients excluding the chicken and olives in a bowl.

2. Add the marinade to the seasoned chicken and keep in the fridge overnight to intensify the flavours.

3. Pick the chicken out of the marinade and roast in the oven with a little olive oil.

4. Drain the liquid from the marinade with a sieve so that the onions remain in the sieve. Bring the liquid to a boil then add the liquid to the chicken which is already cooking.

5. While the chicken is cooking in the oven, take a large pan and fry the onions till they caramelise or are golden in colour.

6. Layer the onions on top of the chicken and then place a few more pieces of chicken on top.

7. Cover the chicken and onion tray with grease proof paper and foil. Braise the chicken for 1 hour at 180 degrees.

8. Remove the foil. Check if the chicken is cooked then add the green olives. Mix the ingredients and cook again for 20 minutes to colour the chicken and to enhance the flavours.

Serve with rice.

CHIPOTLE CHICKEN

Ingredients

1kg of chicken wings or breast
12 pitted dates
2 tbsp dried chipotle chillies
12 tbsp balsamic vinegar
4 tbsp olive oil
1tsp garlic powder
1 tsp smoked paprika
1 tsp cumin powder
Salt and pepper to taste

Directions

1. Blend all the ingredients together, excluding the chicken and mix together with the wings in a bowl, then leave to marinate overnight.

2. Roast at 160C for 30 mins or till golden brown.

3. Once the wings are cooked, increase the oven temperature to 200 degrees and cook for 10 to 15 minutes to brown the chicken further on both sides. If cooking chicken breast, reduce the cooking time by half.

Serve with Mexican rice, guacamole, salsa and black beans.

CHICKEN FAJITAS

Ingredients

2kg chicken thighs, cut into strips and marinated
1/2 tbsp chilli powder
1 tbsp smoked paprika
1 tbsp ground cumin
1 tbsp garlic powder
½ tbsp ground coriander
2 tbsp fresh coriander
3 tbsp olive oil
Juice of 1 lime
Fajita veggie mix
2 red peppers cut into strips
2 green peppers, cut into strips
1 red onion, sliced
1 red chilli, chopped

Directions

1. In a bowl, mix the chicken with spices and lime. Leave to marinate in the fridge overnight.

2. Stir fry the chicken in a pan or cook on a large hot skillet or griddle for 30 to 45 minutes depending on the size of the chicken strips.

3. Toss in the red and green peppers, onion and chilli.

4. Serve on wraps with sour cream and guacamole.

*Note Chicken breast cooks in less time than chicken thighs.

POT ROAST CHICKEN

Ingredients

1 whole chicken 1kg to 2.5kg
Mirepoix vegetables
1 celery
1 carrot
1 medium onion
½ leek
5 garlic cloves
3 thyme sprigs
3 rosemary sprigs
1 bay leaf
600ml chicken stock (see recipe from previous pages)

Directions

1. Remove the wish bone from underneath the breast of the chicken.

2. Season the chicken with salt and pepper.

3. Pull the breast skin under the neck so that the breast isn't exposed during cooking as the meat shrinks.

4. Fry the diced vegetables with the garlic until golden brown, then add the herbs. No need to chop.

5. Layer the vegetables in an oven tray then put the chicken on top.

6. Pour over the stock. Cover the chicken with greaseproof paper, then with foil, tightly.

7. Place the chicken in the oven at 180C for an hour and a half.

8. Uncover the chicken and cook at 200C to colour the chicken.

9. Once the chicken is brown, place on a silver tray loosely covered with foil while you make the

sauce.

10. To make the sauce, pass / strain the stock through a sieve reserving the liquid and not the vegetables. Reduce the stock by simmering while skimming off the debris.

11. Thicken the sauce with a little corn flour paste if required and bring to the boil. The sauce must be brown, glossy and of a pouring consistency. Taste for seasoning. Serve the chicken with the sauce, roast potatoes or mash and roasted vegetables.

WHITE CHICKEN CASSEROLE

Ingredients

1kg of chicken thighs, diced
30g butter
30g flour
500g button mushrooms, washed
600ml double cream
White mirepoix veg
1 celery
1 leek
1 onion
2 garlic cloves, diced
5 sprigs of chopped thyme
1 bay leaf
Salt and pepper to taste

Directions

1. Season the chicken and place in a pot. Cover the chicken with just enough cold water or stock. Bring the chicken to the boil and simmer for about 20 mins removing the debris with a ladle. (Leave the chicken in the liquid once cooked)

2. While the chicken is cooking, in another pan sweat or fry the vegetables in butter but without colouring.

3. Add the mushrooms, cutting into quarters if too large.

4. Add herbs and flour. Cook and stir for 2 minutes then add the cream.

5. Mix the ingredients in the 2 pans together and cook for about 15 minutes or until reduced and thoroughly cooked. The sauce must be white, creamy and flavourful.

6. Garnish the stew with chopped parsley and taste for seasoning. Serve with roasted new potatoes and broccoli.

In Conclusion...

I hope you have enjoyed cooking our stress-free recipes for your friends and family, whilst at the same time thinking about the *ingredients and tools you will need, to achieve your dream and what cooking method you will use.*

Let me encourage you that it's the small steps that count. I learned that; it is the small hinges that swing big doors. Start with the ingredients you have, mise en place and add your *flair* to whatever you do.

From the great motivators such as Benjamin Hardy, I have learned that what is happening in the world today is not happening *to* you, but *for* you.

It's now time to flap your wings and fly!

Remember that your destination is not in the pot, but at the top! You have not come this far to quit.

While you are on your journey of personal development or preparing to launch your new venture, do not forget to serve yourself some tasty chicken with flavours from around the world. Extend your hospitality to your neighbours and community by getting them their own copy of the cookbook. Share the love of cooking and keep seasoning. Motivate yourself like I do daily, shutting down fear and declaring to my inner being and my surroundings- 'yes chic-ken!'

NOTES:

NOTES:

Index

About the author   109

About the book   7

Acknowledgements   8

Aroma   9, 18, 19

Baking   36

Base Recipes   43

BBQ chicken   72

Braised red pepper and tomato chicken   68

Braising   38

Cajun chicken   78

Chicken curry – flavours of Bahia   66

Chicken fajitas   94

Chicken stock   21, 43

Chicken tikka   87

Chicken yassa   89

Chipotle chicken   92

Contents Page   2

Cutting   33

Dry store ingredients   28

Dream   9, 12, 16

Essential   10, 27, 28

Equipment needed   22, 23, 24, 25, 26

Foreword   5

Fried chicken   55

Frying   35

Ginger, honey & soy chicken   47

Griddling   37

Grilling   35

Harissa chicken   80

Herbs   9, 26

In conclusion   101

Introduction   10

Inspirational quotes   40

Jerk style chicken   64

Kitchen tips   39

Lemon & herb chicken   70

Malay chicken curry   74

Marinate   7, 9

Marinating   32

More than a chicken dream   18

Mirepoix   38, 43

My Story   12

Notes   103

Parmesan chicken   51

Peri Peri chicken   76

Pesto chicken   49

Poaching   37

Pot roast chicken   97

Preface   9

Preparation   29

Preparing poultry   31

Recipes   41

Recycling   37

Roast chicken   57

Roasting   36

Salt and pepper chicken   67

Steaming   36

Stewing   38

Stir fry   37

Storing   34

Sunshine chicken   59

Thai flavoured grilled spatchcock chicken   53

Tomato and red pepper sauce   45

Warm chicken and orzo salad   85

Wastage   33

Ways to cook chicken   34

White chicken casserole   99

About the author

Portia is married with three beautiful children. Her eldest child is 20 years old. She is an MMU (Manchester Metropolitan University) graduate. She graduated with a BA Hons degree in Hospitality and Culinary Arts.

Portia is a community chef specialising in food safety, training and teaching cookery life skills as well as spreading the love for food and seasoning. She also works with women in the community using the power of food to break social barriers and change attitudes. Portia is also a professional chef, lecturer, NVQ assessor and caterer.

Get in touch

Email: flaircookery@outlook.com

Instagram: @flaircookery

Facebook:
https://www.facebook.com/groups/259625565241936/

Printed in Great Britain
by Amazon